Jesus My Song!

A Five-Week Devotional for Music Lovers

Tim Wesemann

www.CTAinc.com

Jesus, My Song
A Five-Week Devotional for Music Lovers
by Tim Wesemann
www.timwesemann.com

Copyright © 2006 CTA, Inc.
1625 Larkin Williams Rd.
Fenton, MO 63026-1205

All rights reserved. No part of this publication may be reproduced, stored in a retrieval system, or transmitted, in any form or by any means, electronic, mechanical, photocopying, recording, or otherwise, without the prior written permission of CTA, Inc.

Unless otherwise indicated, all Scripture is from The Holy Bible, English Standard Version, copyright © 2001 by Crossway Bibles, a division of Good News Publishers. Used by permission. All rights reserved.

Scripture quotations so indicated are from **THE MESSAGE**. Copyright © by Eugene H. Peterson 1993, 1994, 1995, 1996, 2000, 2001, 2002. Used by permission of NavPress Publishing Group.

Scripture quotations marked NIV are taken from the HOLY BIBLE, NEW INTERNATIONAL VERSION®. Copyright © 1973, 1978, 1984 International Bible Society. Used by permission of Zondervan. All rights reserved.

Scripture quotations marked NKJV are taken from the New King James Version. Copyright © 1982 by Thomas Nelson, Inc. Used by permission. All rights reserved.

ISBN 1-933234-04-0
PRINTED IN THAILAND

In Terms of Praise

*A crescendo of voices in Heaven sang out,
The kingdom of the world is now
the Kingdom of our God
and his Messiah!
He will rule forever and ever!*

Revelation 11:15 THE MESSAGE

Day 1

Crescendo

Praise God as you read Psalm 150.

Crescendo: Gradually growing louder

The director taps his baton on the music stand. Vocalists straighten their backs and focus all their attention on the one who stands before them. On cue from the director, instruments rise in unison. At just the right moment, the director signals the preparatory beat. The piece begins. Voices and instruments respond with music that brings God glory. As the song continues, the music gradually swells in a breathtaking crescendo of praise.

Sound familiar? Members of choirs, orchestras, bands, bell choirs, and other musical groups certainly identify with the picture described above. As Christian musicians or simply as Christians who love music, we can also identify with another, similar picture.

The Director cues the musicians from his throne. Filled with his gift of music, his people and his holy angels straighten their backs, raise their expectations, and focus on the One who stands before them. At just the right moment, the Director signals. The "peace" begins. Music from heaven and earth fills the universe in response to God's gift of a Savior, the Son who brings his Father glory and the Father's sinful children forgiveness and salvation. As the life-song continues, the sounds of thanksgiving and joy progressively swell, forming an eternal, breathtaking crescendo of praise.

Prayers arise before God's throne of grace, asking that the Holy Spirit work through his Word and this devotional to strengthen faith and create lives that sing praise—a crescendo of praise—to Jesus, our Song and Salvation.

Praise the Lord! Praise him throughout the universe! Praise him for all he has done and will do! As we grow in his love, may our praise grow as the music builds and all our songs combine to create a richly textured hymn of thanks in perfect harmony! Let everything that has breath praise the Lord! Praise the Lord!

Let everything that has breath praise the LORD!
Psalm 150:6

Prayer suggestion: Lord, compose a crescendo of praise within my life in response to the peace you have written on my heart through your gift of salvation in Jesus Christ. I praise you, Lord! Amen.

Day 2

Pianissimo

Praise God as you read Psalm 119:27–28.

Pianissimo: Very soft

As our crescendo of praise builds in the presence of Jesus, our Song, let us focus our attention today on the musical notation *pianissimo*.

When the Holy Spirit created faith within you, did he summon you with the same fanfare he used to get Saul's attention (Acts 9:1–19)? Or did he use a pianissimo event, similar to the one the Ethiopian treasurer experienced (Acts 8:26–39)? For the majority of us, I imagine the pianissimo more likely describes our faith journey. While many of us may look for or perhaps even hope for God's thunderous, booming call, God often speaks in the soft, gentle whisper of grace.

How often the crescendo of praise we sing in Spirit-created faith begins with quiet times of reflection or confession as we
- read from a Bible tucked away in the drawer of a hotel room's bedside table;
- recall the person who first told us about Jesus' story and the Savior's subsequent effect on our life's story;
- rejoice over the waters of Baptism;
- listen to a Christian radio station;

- utter humble prayers of confession during a long walk;
- hear the words, "I love you and I forgive you" softly spoken into our ears;
- *(add your own)*

_____

_____

Psalm 119:27–28 reminds us that it is good to quietly ponder God's miracle-wonders as he softly whispers in our ears, "I love you. I forgive you. I will never leave you or forsake you, my dearly loved child."

> *Softly and tenderly Jesus is calling . . .*
> *Come home, come home,*
> *You who are weary, come home;*
> *Earnestly, tenderly, Jesus is calling,*
> *Calling, O sinner, come home!*

Will L. Thompson

Strengthen me according to your word!
Psalm 119:28

Prayer suggestion: Thank you for pursuing me, Jesus, and meeting me—even when I'm deep in the mire of sin, even in times when guilt speaks loudly, and also in those times of humble reflection and quiet confession. Your pianissimo love plays out loudly in my life! Amen.

Day 3

Forte

Praise God as you read Psalm 100.

Forte: Loud, strong

Recall the loudest environment you've ever experienced. We've probably all found our ears ringing at a party; on the factory floor; at a rock concert; during a coworker's temper tantrum; or when an animal barks, squeaks, or roars.

We don't usually link *loud* experiences and *praise*. In fact, for some of us, at least part of the time, our false piety and the sinful form of pride keep us from letting loose and raising the roof in praise to God! But today I encourage you to start praising your Savior in the same way you will one day when in heaven before his throne. As you imagine that day, consider the fact that *loud* appears twenty-one times in the book of Revelation! Loud voices. Loud shouts. Loud noises. All describe the worship of the heavenly Jerusalem.

When David assigned the Levites to serve as musicians (1 Chronicles 15:16), he told them to sing and "play loudly on musical instruments, on harps and lyres and cymbals, to raise sounds of joy!" If you don't think the psalmist promoted loud praise, try reading Psalm 100 in a praise-filled way while using a quiet, mumbling voice. It's tough to do! The psalm cries out, asking of us a loud voice of joy and praise!

Make a joyful noise to the LORD, all the earth!
Serve the LORD with gladness!
Come into his presence with singing!
Know that the LORD, he is God!
It is he who made us, and we are his;
we are his people, and the sheep of his pasture.
Enter his gates with thanksgiving,
and his courts with praise!
Give thanks to him; bless his name!
For the LORD is good;
his steadfast love endures forever,
and his faithfulness to all generations.

As God writes the musical score of our lives, notice he has handwritten *forte* with his own blood all over the manuscript. Our Savior deserves our loud praises not only in heaven but also on this side of paradise!

The LORD is good.
Psalm 100:5

Prayer suggestion: Savior, forgive me for my timid and limited praise. Forgive the sinful pride and false piety that prevent me from loudly and freely praising your name. From the cross you called out in a *loud* voice, "Father, into your hands I commit my spirit!" Standing beneath that cross in worship, that is my prayer too. Amen.

Day 4

Virtuoso

Praise God as you read Psalm 42:4.

*Virtuoso: A person with notable technical skill
in the performance of music*

Are you gifted as a virtuoso—blessed with great skills for the performance of music? Or do you know someone whom you consider a very gifted musician?

The superscription "To the Choirmaster" stands out above the words of Psalm 42 in my Bible. Maybe it could read, "To the Virtuoso." The psalm writer has a heavy heart. He feels less than a spiritual virtuoso as he writes. He's depressed and spiritually dry.

Eugene Peterson, in *The Message*, paraphrases some of the psalmist's opening words:

> *A white-tailed deer drinks from the creek;*
> *I want to drink God, deep draughts of God. . . .*
> *I'm on a diet of tears—*
> *tears for breakfast, tears for supper. . . .*
> *These are the things I go over and over,*
> *emptying out the pockets of my life.*
> *I was always at the head of the worshiping crowd, right out in front,*
> *Leading them all, eager to arrive and worship,*

*Shouting praises, singing thanksgiving—
celebrating, all of us, God's feast!*

The writer wants to sing praises, but he's frustrated with the way he feels. The psalmist used to be at the head of the worshiping crowd, leading them all in praise. Now his praise pockets are empty.

It's true: a virtuoso wears out. Psalm writers find their energy drained. Musicians travel through dry spiritual deserts. We have all experienced them too.

But notice the heart of the writer. He wants, longs, yearns to drink deep draughts of God. He knows the One who brings God-honoring music back into his life is the Lord of the Universe, the true spiritual virtuoso whose gifts exceed mere notability. We stand in awe of him and his gifts. We drink deeply of his goodness so our mouths can sing again as he restores joy to our souls! Come, drink of God—then thank the Lord with the gift of music!

With glad shouts and songs of praise . . .
Psalm 42:4

Prayer suggestion: Jesus, you are my true Song. You put a song of life in me, and I want to sing it. When I feel spiritually dry, lead me to your springs of living water and quench my thirst, so I can worship you joyfully in music and in everything else I do! I give you praise while I pray in your holy name! Amen.

Day 5

Expressionism

Praise God as you read Psalm 13.

Expressionism: A tonal and violent style used as a means of evoking heightened emotions and states of mind

Many songs we know as psalms might fall into the category of *Expressionism*. The psalms teem with emotion while touching our own. The words often uncover the heart of the psalmist—his frustrations and complaints, as well as his thankfulness and praise. The psalmists invite us to travel with them on their roller coaster rides through life.

For example, David's Psalm 13 begins with a harsh—almost violent—expression of frustration with God, whom he feels has abandoned him. David's accusations and questions continue throughout the first four verses.

Do you ever feel you've recently boarded a roller coaster of frustrations and will explode unless you can find a way to express them? Is your list of *God questions* growing long?

- Lord, I'm tired of practicing the same music week after week. How long until the joy returns?
- Lord, I feel so unappreciated. Have *you* forgotten me too?

- Lord, I struggle to share my music with *you know who*. Did you arrange our seating chart for your own entertainment?
- Lord, I can't concentrate here! Can't you do something about all this disharmony at home?

David's frustrations mirror our own. But after expressing those frustrations, David takes a deep breath and allows the Holy Spirit to fill his lungs and heart with fresh hope. The Lord quiets him with love and points him to the truth. Then David's heart sings. Our Spirit-filled hearts echo his song.

But I have trusted in your steadfast love;
My heart shall rejoice in your salvation.
*I will sing to the L*ORD*,*
because he has dealt bountifully with me.
Psalm 13:5–6

Prayer suggestion: Pray the verses above, pausing after each line for personal reflection.

Days 6-7
Time for Reflection
In Terms of Praise

As I meditate on this week's theme and Scriptures, these are the things . . .

1. for which I want to give praise to my Savior-God;
2. I have learned about my Lord and my life through these devotional studies;
3. I need the Holy Spirit's help to change within my life; and
4. I want to share with others, so they might praise Jesus, their Song and Salvation.

Voices of Praise

*My heart is steadfast, O God!
I will sing and make melody
with all my being!*

Psalm 108:1

Day 8

Trio

Praise God as you read 2 Corinthians 13:14.

Trio: A composition written for three voices or instruments and performed by three persons

They have become known as *The Three Tenors*—José Carreras, Plácido Domingo, and Luciano Pavarotti. The fame of each spans the globe. Each brings his own extraordinary individual gifts to a trio, all the while working in concert with the other two. A list of the trio's accomplishments could fill a book.

Though famous, gifted, and respected, this trio doesn't even come close to the majesty, fame, and honor due another "trio." Known throughout the universe, each brings extraordinary individual gifts, all the while working in perfect concert with the others. A list of this trio's accomplishments *does* fill a book! Of course I'm referring to *The Holy Trinity*—Father, Son, and Holy Spirit.

One God—three distinct persons in one divine being.
- The Father—Creator, Provider, and Protector
- The Son—Jesus Christ, Redeemer, Savior
- The Holy Spirit—Faith Creator and Sustainer, Comforter

What a trio, one like no other! Its gifts astonishing—to say the least. The blessing sometimes known as Paul's benediction outlines the gifts this God-Trio promises to all:

- The amazing grace of Jesus, our Savior.
- The extravagant love of the Father.
- The intimate companionship of the Holy Spirit.

Let your Three-in-One God orchestrate those notes on the staff of your life today as you then respond with a lifelong love song to the Trio like no other.

The grace of the Lord Jesus Christ and the love of God
and the fellowship of the Holy Spirit
be with you all.
2 Corinthians 13:14

Prayer suggestion: Father, Son, and Holy Spirit, I humbly praise your name and stand in awe of your grace, your love, and your companionship. Teach me to live in harmony with your will. Amen.

Day 9

A capella

Praise God as you read Psalm 145:1–2.

A cappella: One or more vocalists performing without accompaniment

What comes to mind when you think of the phrase *one-on-one time* with God, our heavenly Father?

- Taking a walk and having a talk with God?
- Spending time in private Bible study or devotions?
- Driving alone while singing Christian songs?
- Sitting silently in the middle of God's creation, soaking in the blessing of his presence?
- Letting your heart pray and praise anywhere, anytime?

Are we ever truly without accompaniment when we worship the Lord? Does one-on-one time with God really exist? Think about it.

Even when we find ourselves in complete solitude—worshiping him, talking to him, praising him—we don't truly worship *a cappella*, without accompaniment.

Consider these passages and draw your own conclusions:

> *If we don't know how or what to pray, it doesn't matter. [The Holy Spirit] does our praying in and for us, making prayer out of our wordless sighs, our aching groans. He knows us far better than we know ourselves . . . and keeps us present before God.*
> Romans 8:26–27 THE MESSAGE

> *Are not all angels ministering spirits sent to serve those who will inherit salvation?*
> Hebrews 1:14 NIV

> *Therefore, since we are surrounded by such a great cloud of witnesses, . . . let us run with perseverance the race marked out for us.*
> Hebrews 12:1 NIV

May remembering that cloud of faithful witnesses and all the holy angels surrounding you help you treasure your "one-on-one time" with your Savior even more!

I will extol you, my God and King.
Psalm 145:1

Prayer suggestion: Holy Spirit, shape the prayer-songs of my heart and mouth to form a perfect anthem of praise and present it to the Father's throne of grace in Jesus' precious name. Amen.

Day 10

Unison

Praise God as you read John 17:20–26.

Unison: Two or more voices or instruments playing the same note simultaneously

Christians gather each weekend in church and blend their voices to sing in perfect unison. Too bad those same Christians can't live in perfect unison throughout the week!

Petty arguments and conflicts within the body of believers in our own congregation can frustrate us. We sometimes wonder why the leaders of the church at large seem to lose focus. We scratch our heads trying to figure out why the Christian church has one Lord and Savior but so many different beliefs, all taken from one Bible!

The night before Jesus was crucified, he prayed to his Father, offering petitions for himself, for his disciples, and for all believers (John 17). He prayed for unity among his followers—ourselves included (John 17:20–26). How close have we come? Perhaps not very.

Jesus continues to sing a song of unity today:

> *Lay your jealousy, anger, and pride*
> *at my cross;*

Know only me—
consider everything else a loss;
Open your fists and I'll join your hands in unity;
I'll take your sins and set you free . . .
In unity you'll live—
I've set you free. I've set you free!

Our Savior's heart sings of unity among his people. His forgiveness makes that unity possible. And one day, by grace through faith in Jesus, we'll sing and live in *perfect* unison. No instruments playing out of tune. No voices sounding just a tad flat. No divisions in choirs or bands. Nothing but God's children singing and playing in unison, giving the King the praise due his name.

Even now, we hear in the distance heaven's music, a song of perfect, undivided love. Keep listening! One day all of us who believe in Jesus as the Savior will live, sing, and play in perfect unison! Thank you, Jesus!

That they may all be one . . .
John 17:21

Prayer suggestion: Father God, you give endurance and encouragement. Grant us a spirit of unity as we follow our Savior, Jesus Christ, so that with one heart and mouth we will glorify you now and forever. Amen.

Day 11

Falsetto

Praise God as you read Proverbs 16:13.

Falsetto: A style of male singing by which, with partial use of the vocal chords, the voice is able to reach the pitch of a female voice

At choir rehearsals you'll find me in the tenor section. When the director distributes a new piece of music, I immediately check to see how high the notes for the tenor part climb. Will I need my falsetto voice? I don't appreciate having to twist my vocal chords around. (Okay, I'm exaggerating.) But I don't enjoy singing notes so high I might be mistaken for the soprano in the front row!

As a matter of fact, I personally don't enjoy singing in my falsetto voice at all. Is it really *my* voice? It just doesn't sound right to me.

Do you feel comfortable using a false voice? Before you answer, consider the fact that most of us use a false voice all the time, but not when we're standing on choir risers. All of us sometimes twist the voice of truth a little. Soon little white *falsetto* lies come out of our mouths! Or maybe we hide behind masks, allowing people to think things are going great in our lives while we know that's not the true story.

A false voice here, a false voice there—does it really matter? According to wise King Solomon's words in Proverbs 16:13:

> *Righteous lips are the delight of a king, and he loves him who speaks what is right.*

Tenors, even those using falsetto voices, can and do sing sincere praise to the Father. But a false voice, a lying tongue, an anxious heart trying to hide from God—none of these honor the Father. How thankful we are, knowing that Jesus Christ sang a song of sacrifice on that Friday centuries ago! Now forgiveness fills the staff lines of our lives. Christ's righteousness has become the melody of our lives, a melody that delights the King of kings!

Righteous lips are the delight of a king.
Proverbs 16:13

Prayer suggestion: Lord Jesus Christ, forgive me when I bear false witness, speak half-truths or blatant lies, trust false gods, ignore your Word of truth, give people false impressions, or allow my lips, mind, or actions to sing anything but your truth. Grant me righteous lips to sing your praise! Amen.

Day 12

Tessitura

Praise God as you read Psalm 119:147–149.

Tessitura: The range of an instrumental or vocal part

Even among musicians, *tessitura* isn't a common term. It refers to range. The notes on a musical score can take a musician from very high notes to deep, low tones. But voices and instruments have limited range. Sopranos aren't going to hit the notes familiar to a bass vocalist. A piccolo and a sousaphone differ markedly in appearance and in musical range.

Like voices and instruments, people, too, vary in *tessitura*. Some of us enjoy a wider range of skills than others, but no matter how gifted we are, those gifts have limits. Despite people who think they know it all, no human brain can answer every question.

Our experiences with limitations can limit our spiritual vision and our courage when it comes to serving those around us. We may feel the Spirit tugging our hand, encouraging us to serve. Being ever aware of our limitations, we might find ourselves tugging back, eager to stay on safe ground. But in times like that we need to remember there is no limit to what can be done in duet with Christ!

- There is no limit to the praise that can be offered to our heavenly Father as Christ sings with us!
- There is no limit to our service when Jesus takes the role of Concertmaster!
- There is no limit to the joy and peace that play constantly in our lives when we live in harmony with the Prince of Peace!

Hear my voice according to your steadfast love.
Psalm 119:149

Prayer suggestion: It's such a blessing to sing or play duets with you, Jesus! You are my Song! Teach me to hit new heights and maneuver smoothly through the depths. You give me so many reasons to praise your holy name! Amen and Amen! Alleluia!

Days 13-14
Time for Reflection
Voices of Praise

As I meditate on this week's theme and Scriptures, these are the things . . .

1. for which I want to give praise to my Savior-God;
2. I have learned about my Lord and my life through these devotional studies;
3. I need the Holy Spirit's help to change within my life; and
4. I want to share with others, so they might praise Jesus, their Song and Salvation.

Notes of Praise

Thank GOD! Call out his Name!
Tell the whole world who he is and what he's done!
Sing to him! Play songs for him!
Broadcast all his wonders!

Sing to GOD, everyone and everything!
Get out his salvation news every day!

1 Chronicles 16:8–9, 23 THE MESSAGE

Day 15

Harmony

Praise God as you read Romans 15:5–6.

Harmony: Pleasing combination of two or three tones played together in the background while a melody is being played

In *The Message*, Eugene Peterson beautifully paraphrases Paul's words:

May our dependably steady and warmly
personal God develop maturity in you so
that you get along with each other as well as
Jesus gets along with us all. Then we'll be a choir—
not our voices only, but our very lives
singing in harmony in a stunning anthem
to the God and Father of our Master Jesus!
Romans 15:5–6 THE MESSAGE

Let's practice singing this score a few measures at a time.

- Paul describes God as "dependably steady" and "warmly personal." In a world with little that's dependable or steady, we can count on him! Neither ways nor words will change. Real. Personal. Real personal! Up and close and warmly personal—that's our Savior!

- God matures our faith, teaching us how to put the needs of others above our own. That maturity animates our performance; it orchestrates our ability to play in unison as God's people.
- We move from chanting in unison to a full choir—all of us singing with voices and lives praising God *in harmony*—lifting up a stunning anthem!

Once again, from the beginning . . . God doesn't change. We can depend on him. He loves us and knows each of us intimately. The Holy Spirit grows our faith. In doing so, he brings God's people together with one voice. As maturity increases, the crescendo of praise grows. Suddenly we find we've become a full choir, voices and joyous lives singing praise to God in perfect harmony!

Once again, from the beginning, this time in harmony . . .

May the God of endurance and encouragement grant you to live in such harmony with one another, in accord with Christ Jesus, that together you may with one voice glorify the God and Father of our Lord Jesus Christ.
Romans 15:5–6

Prayer suggestion: Pray the message of Romans 15:5–6.

Day 16

Glissando

Praise God as you read Romans 7:18–20.

Glissando: Sliding between two notes

A musical term, *glissando* also describes a spiritual phenomenon. In Romans 7:13–20, Paul confesses that a lot of *glissando-ing* (Yes, I just made up that word!) goes on in his life—a lot of sliding from tone to tone. We'd do well to confess the same thing. In music, *glissando* adds beauty. But *glissando* in our life's score is less than beautiful.

Glissando refers to the sliding between two notes or tones. Daily we find ourselves sliding between the unwavering notes of our Lord's faithfulness and our own notes of unfaithfulness. We slide between this note and that, seeking to please ourselves or other human beings. We seek out melodies that will soothe our itching ears. Often those notes don't harmonize with God's will for our lives.

We slide so easily from . . .
- a loving tone to a tone of hatred;
- a peaceful note to a note of chaos;
- a calming tone to one filled with anger;
- a note of servanthood to a note of greed;
- a forgiving tone to a tone of revenge.

Paul writes:

> *For I know that nothing good dwells in me, that is, in my flesh. For I have the desire to do what is right, but not the ability to carry it out. For I do not do the good I want, but the evil I do not want is what I keep on doing.*
>
> *Romans 7:18–19*

We have such great plans. We want to follow God's sheet music just as he composed it, but soon we find ourselves sliding into our own renditions that fall flat of God's glory. Where's the hope? Slide down a few verses in Romans 7 to verses 24 and 25, where Paul writes,

> *Wretched man that I am! Who will deliver me from this body of death? Thanks be to God through Jesus Christ our Lord!*

There's our hope!

> ***For I have the desire to do what is right,***
> ***but not the ability to carry it out.***
> ***Romans 7:18***

Prayer suggestion: Lord, I want to follow you with all my heart. But what I want to do, I often do not do! The evil I do not want is what I keep on doing! Lord, have mercy on me, a sinner. Wretched, I fall at the foot of your cross, relying fully on your mercy and forgiveness. Thanks be to God through Jesus Christ who has delivered me, saved me, forgiven me, and set me free to serve him and his people! Amen!

Day 17

Chord

Praise God as you read Ephesians 5:18–21.

Chord: Three or more notes played simultaneously in harmony

A pianist plays a chord with one hand. A bell choir needs several different bells to play a chord. A guitar player uses both hands to play both minor chords and major chords ranging from the simple to the complex.

In Ephesians 5:18–21, Paul plays for us the *major* chords in a Christian's life. We might title the first chord "Love One Another." Here, Paul encourages us to talk to one another of God's love, playing in these three notes and simultaneously in harmony:

psalms,
hymns,
and spiritual songs

Blended together, these make sweet music with which we can uplift one another. Then Paul moves to another chord, the major chord for a song that could be titled "Love the Lord."

Listen to the symmetry of this major chord:
> *singing,*
> *making melodies (to the Lord),*
> *and always giving thanks*

Note upon note, all giving glory to the Father in the name of our Lord Jesus Christ as we willingly submit to one another out of reverence for Christ!

The beauty of these chords lies in their harmony. One brother or sister in Christ encourages someone with a psalm, another with a hymn, and another with a spiritual song. No note or person deems itself more important than another; all work together, playing in harmony. The same is true for worship—one sings, another reads, still another testifies, and all give thanks. No one is more important than the others; all work together, in harmony, to give God the glory he deserves!

Be filled with the Spirit, addressing one another in psalms and hymns and spiritual songs, singing and making melody to the Lord with all your heart.
Ephesians 5:18–19

Prayer suggestion: Pray a favorite hymn, psalm, or spiritual song in honor of Jesus your Song!

Day 18

Drone

Praise God as you read Psalm 32:1–5, 11.

Drone: Dull, monotonous tone such as a humming or buzzing sound or a bass note held under a melody

As the body of Christ gathers together in the house of God each week, perhaps you find yourself on occasion taking time to drone? David knows about droning. He droned on and on after his affair with Bathsheba, as for months he refused to repent. Although David uses different terms, he describes his lack of repentance this way:

For when I kept silent, my bones wasted away through my groaning all day long. For day and night your hand was heavy upon me; my strength was dried up as by the heat of summer.
Psalm 32:3–4

While the melody of life played on among the Lord's repentant people, David's guilt droned on in sharp contrast, sounding a monotonous bass note. That dull tone betrayed the state of his soul. He had sinned and his impenitence sapped his joy. Can you relate? I know I can!

Now let's head back into our Sabbath worship. Walking through the doors of the church you'll find experts gifted in droning. Their faces may not show it, but they harbor secret sin and guilt on the inside. What better place than the house of God, filled with both fellow droners and the grace of our Savior, to confess our sins and receive God's full forgiveness.

When David kept silent, the droning note of despair filled his body. But when he acknowledged his sin to the Lord and stopped trying to cover it up, he received the free and freeing gift of forgiveness. Then his soul could sing a new song of thanks and praise (Psalm 32:4–5, 11).

One last note. If you happen to hear a monotonous groaning tone of guilt reverberating on your own soul, you need not wait for the next scheduled worship service to find relief. God's forgiveness is here for you right now. Go ahead, confess your sin. You can't hide it from him. Lay it at Jesus' cross. You've been forgiven and saved by the blood of the Lamb! Away with the groaning and droning! Bring on the thanksgiving and praise!

> *Be glad in the LORD, and rejoice.*
> *Psalm 32:11*

Prayer suggestion: Pray words of confession and then listen as the Lord says, "Your sins are forgiven; I will remember them no more."

Day 19

Accent

Praise God as you read Matthew 26:73.

Accent: Stress of one tone over others making it stand out; often the first beat of a measure

God places accent marks over all the lives of his people. The major accent comes as the Holy Spirit creates faith within us. Think about it! God created you, chose you, forgave you, and adopted you into his family! He has declared you holy in the holiness Christ Jesus won for you on Calvary's cross.

Besides all this, the Lord also has accented your life with a variety of gifts and talents that make it possible for you to serve him and his people. He accents his people with gifts of musicianship, leadership, intellect, athleticism, a passion for prayer, great capacity for compassion, teaching, preaching, evangelism, craftsmanship, and so much more! God gifts each of us though none of us deserve it.

Matthew 26:73 uses the word *accent,* but outside a musical context. Yet the point seems so appropriate I can't pass it up! The term appears in the story of Peter's denial of Jesus. Servants and bystanders in the courtyard recognize Peter as a disciple, yet he denies knowing Jesus. One of them says to him, "Certainly you too are one of them, for your accent gives you away."

That verse sparked a thought for me that applies to our conversation. I wonder if our *accent* gives us away to others? Does the accent of Jesus Christ living within us tell others that we walk with Jesus? Do others see the God-placed accents and gifts in our lives and, in response, do they give God the glory? In light of those questions, consider these words of Jesus:

Let your light shine before others, so that they may see your good works and give glory to your Father who is in heaven.

Matthew 5:16

Paul writes:

For I am not ashamed of the gospel, for it is the power of God for salvation to everyone who believes.

Romans 1:16

Your accent betrays you.
Matthew 26:73

Prayer suggestion: Holy Spirit, your accent mark of faith is upon me! Thank you, Spirit! Jesus, your accent mark of salvation is upon me. I give you thanks, my Savior. Father, you have created me with accents of unique giftedness marking my life. I thank you. I pray you will use all these accents, my Lord, to bring honor and glory to your name. Amen.

Days 20-21
Time for Reflection
Notes of Praise

As I meditate on this week's theme and Scriptures, these are the things . . .

1. for which I want to give praise to my Savior-God;
2. I have learned about my Lord and my life through these devotional studies;
3. I need the Holy Spirit's help to change within my life; and
4. I want to share with others, so they might praise Jesus, their Song and Salvation.

Rhythms of Praise

Let the peace of Christ rule in your hearts, to which indeed you were called in one body. And be thankful. Let the word of Christ dwell in you richly, teaching and admonishing one another in all wisdom, singing psalms and hymns and spiritual songs, with thankfulness in your hearts to God. And whatever you do, in word or deed, do everything in the name of the Lord Jesus, giving thanks to God the Father through him.

Colossians 3:15–17

Day 22

Tempo

Praise God as you read Romans 12:2.

Tempo: The speed at which music is or ought to be played

Musicians, under the direction of a conductor or director, follow the tempo indicated on a piece of music. But how do *we* decide on the tempo of our days? God has given us free will to choose our pace. Too often, I'm afraid, we listen to the tempting tempos of the world around us and conform our tempo to its tempo. We want to blend in.

Some days, we attempt to keep in time with those speeding through life, grabbing all the sixteenth notes we can, enjoying every trill and thrill! Some days we choose the slow, lazy tempo of those around us in the world, unmoved by the needs that Jesus, in love, would have us meet. We sleep during stanzas and complain through refrains.

What tempo have you chosen for the week? Fast? Slow? In-between? As God's people in Christ, we have another option. We can choose the tempo our Director has designated for us. The Holy Spirit writes through the apostle Paul:

Do not be conformed to this world, but be transformed by the renewal of your mind, that by testing you may discern what is the will of God, what is good and acceptable and perfect.

Romans 12:2

Our days will include measures we play and live at a fast tempo and others we live at a much slower pace. Our Director-Savior may have us run to someone who needs our time, our compassionate heart, or God's saving news. Or he may direct us to run quickly into his own arms in order that we might slow the tempo down—to find rest, peace, and comfort in him.

Instead of conforming our lives to the tempo of the world around you, let the Holy Spirit confirm God's direction in your heart and mind, affirming in you the tempo of his good, acceptable, and perfect will.

Be transformed by the renewal of your mind,
that by testing you may discern what is the will of God,
what is good and acceptable and perfect.
Romans 17:2

Prayer suggestion: Holy Spirit, conform my life to the perfect tempo of your own heartbeat. When you lead me at a faster tempo, I pray for endurance and strength. When you direct me to slow down, grant me wisdom and peace, as I rest, content, in you. In Jesus' name. Amen.

Day 23

Adagio

Praise God as you read Matthew 11:28–30

Adagio: A tempo having slow movement; restful; at ease

This moment has *adagio* written all over it. Slow down and let your body, mind, and soul rest in the following words of peace from Scripture. Let God's Word and his presence soothe you. Crawl into your Savior's arms. Rest your head on his shoulder. God's peace *is* with you. Listen as he speaks his *adagio* calm over your life . . .

> *[Jesus said,] Peace I leave with you;*
> *my peace I give to you.*
> *Not as the world gives do I give to you.*
> *Let not your hearts be troubled,*
> *neither let them be afraid.*
>
> John 14:27

> *Be still, and know that I am God.*
> *I will be exalted among the nations,*
> *I will be exalted in the earth!*
> *The LORD of hosts is with us;*
> *The God of Jacob is our fortress.*
>
> Psalm 46:10–11

*[Jesus said,] "Are you tired? Worn out?
Burned out on religion?
Come to me. Get away with me and you'll recover your life. I'll show
you how to take a real rest.
Walk with me and work with me—
watch how I do it.
Learn the unforced rhythms of grace.
I won't lay anything heavy or ill-fitting on you.
Keep company with me and you'll learn to live freely and lightly."
Matthew 11:28–30 THE MESSAGE*

*The LORD bless you and keep you;
The LORD make his face shine upon you
and be gracious to you;
the LORD turn his face toward you
and give you peace.*

Numbers 6:24–26 NIV

You will find rest for your souls.
Matthew 11:29

Prayer suggestion: Peace. I hear you speak it to my heart, my Lord, even as your peace settles over my whole being. You forgive my sins. You strengthen my faith. You quiet me with your love. I am at peace. Thank you, Jesus, my Song of peace. Amen.

Day 24

Allegro

Praise God as you read Isaiah 55:1–13.

Allegro: A direction to play lively and fast

Daily challenges often compel us to shift from an *adagio* pace to an *allegro* one—from a slow, easy tempo to a lively, fast-paced one! That's life! That's reality! But our Lord assures us that however fast-paced life becomes, his *adagio* peace plays for us eternally as well.

God often directed the inspired writers of Scripture to write with a sense of urgency—drafting lively messages that required an immediate response from his people. In many of those passages he directs our tempo still today also.

Consider how much time we spend rushing to save time or money while never giving a thought to the urgency of bringing someone near us to Jesus. Throwing caution to the four winds, we drive faster when the green light turns yellow. Yet when God gives us the go-ahead to share his love with someone, we are so often quick to hit the brakes. We speed past Scripture passages that urgently ask us to tell others of God's saving Word, while we instead slow down to focus only on those words that comfort us personally.

God's Word tells us:

Go therefore and make disciples of all nations.

Matthew 28:19

Blessed is the one who reads aloud the words of this prophecy, and blessed are those who hear, and who keep what is written in it, for the time is near.

Revelation 1:3

Seek the LORD while he may be found; call upon him while he is near.

Isaiah 55:6

With an *allegro*-like urgency, let's run to Christ's cross to receive forgiveness for our past failures. May he renew in us a Spirit-directed desire to share his saving song of salvation with the world!

> ***My word . . . shall not return to me empty,***
> ***but it shall accomplish that which I purpose.***
> ***Isaiah 55:11***

Prayer suggestion: Forgive me, Jesus, for times I've ignored your direction to share your saving news. Stir a passion within my heart to see the needs of others and respond, under your direction. Amen.

Day 25

Legato

Praise God as you read Isaiah 40:1–5.

Legato: Direction to indicate the movement or composition is to be played smoothly

When an orchestra or band tunes up in preparation for a performance, we hear a dreadful mumbo-jumbo of noise! But things change when the director takes his place and raises his hands. At the cue of the director, the first note resounds and the rough, discordant jumble at once becomes a masterful, smooth, flowing composition, pleasing to the ear.

When *legato* is written on the score, musicians play the movement or composition smoothly. Is *legato* written on your day . . . or your life? So few things seem to move smoothly. It's been that way ever since Eden's fruit tempted Adam and Eve into rebelling against their Creator. Down through history since then, even God's people have faced rough times. At just such a time in the history of his people Judah the Lord raised his right hand of truth and wrote *LEGATO!* all over the book of the prophet Isaiah:

Comfort, comfort my people . . . prepare the way of the LORD; make straight in the desert a highway for our God. Every valley shall be lifted up, and every mountain and hill be made low; the uneven ground shall become level, and the rough places a plain. And the glory of the LORD shall be revealed.

from Isaiah 40:1–5

What obstacles clutter your life? What uneven ground needs to be leveled so that the King of glory can reveal himself in you and through you?

In love, God doesn't leave you to smooth the rough edges in your own wisdom or energy. He surrounds you with his instruments of peace—his Word, his forgiveness, his grace, his people. The Director of all life who can calm hurricane-force gales with his *Legato!* (Mark 4:35–39), gracefully lifts his hands to conduct your life moment by moment, creating a symphony of praise.

While his hands were first raised, the world nailed them to a cross. Yet your Savior-Director did not allow the music to come to an end. His Easter victory calms every storm in our lives. Still today, *"Legato! Legato!"* he calls to all musicians following his lead. In his will, his love, we find our peace.

Comfort, comfort my people, says your God.
Isaiah 40:1

Prayer suggestion: Smooth out the rough places in my life, Lord. Lead me to repent of those attitudes and activities by which I make life rough for myself and those around me. Even in those rough times, I thank you for making the road to your cross smooth so I may walk it daily to receive mercy and forgiveness. Amen.

Day 26

Ostinato

Praise God as you read Ephesians 4:32.

Ostinato: A repeated melodic or rhythmic fragment

Sometimes our days pass by like unfinished products on a factory line conveyor belt—repetition is the melody we play. We get up at the same time; use the same toothpaste; eat the same cereal; drive the same route to work or school; see the same people; work the same job; shop at the same stores; watch the same TV shows; read the same e-mails forwarded to us over and over; pull the same bed sheets over our heads; and fall asleep at the same time. Repetition. Repetition. Repetition. Blah. Blah. Blah.

But consider your life as a child of God. The Christian life includes some melodies that grow more beloved, more comforting each time we repeat them. What a joy to be welcomed repeatedly into the throne room of God to . . .

- repent of our sins;
- receive God's full forgiveness through Jesus Christ;
- humbly offer our praises to his holy name;
- hear and study his Word while he grows our faith;
- give thanks for his presence in our lives; and
- confidently offer him our prayers.

What a joy to be repeatedly called upon to be his ambassadors in the world . . .

- forgiving others as Christ has forgiven us;
- sharing the compassionate heart of Jesus with the hurting;
- extending a hand of friendship to the lonely;
- telling the lost of salvation through Christ alone;
- giving hope through Christ for those who struggle; and
- setting an example of Christ's love for those around us.

Repetition. Repetition. Repetition. It makes our lives and hearts sing!

Be kind to one another, tenderhearted, forgiving one another, as God in Christ forgave you.
Ephesians 4:32

Prayer suggestion: Lord, complacency comes easily for us. Bring us joy in living for you and with you day after day after day. Amen!

Days 27-28
Time for Reflection
Rhythms of Praise

As I meditate on this week's theme and Scriptures,
these are the things . . .

1. for which I want to give praise to my Savior-God;
2. I have learned about my Lord and my life through these devotional studies;
3. I need the Holy Spirit's help to change within my life; and
4. I want to share with others, so they might praise Jesus, their Song and Salvation.

Instruments of Praise

Shout your praise to GOD, everybody!
Let loose and sing! Strike up the band!

Round up an orchestra to play for GOD,
Add on a hundred-voice choir.

Feature trumpets and big trombones,
Fill the air with praise to King GOD.

Let the sea and its fish give a round of applause,
With everything living on earth
joining in.

Let ocean breakers call out, "Encore!"
And mountains harmonize the finale—

A tribute to GOD when he comes,
When he comes to set the earth right.

Psalm 98:4–9 THE MESSAGE

Day 29

Conductor

Praise God as you read Psalm 31:3–5.

Conductor: One who directs a group of performers and indicates the tempo, phrasing, dynamics, and style by gestures and facial expressions

Those who conduct choirs or symphony orchestras here on earth indicate the tempo, phrasing, dynamics, and style, pulling the very best possible performances from the artists who work with them. How? They devise a system of gestures and facial expressions to communicate just what the performers need to know and do. I've observed some conductors use dramatic and very pronounced gestures and facial expressions.

All this suggests an interesting thought as we consider Jesus, the Ultimate Conductor. What gestures or facial expressions do you suppose the Conductor uses as he directs our lives?

- Does *the* Conductor smile broadly right now, and in doing so, encourage us to smile—to show that we own the joy of the Lord? Do the facial features of our Savior include prominent laugh lines?
- Does he wave his arms, look, tilt his head, and point in another direction while motioning with his head and eyes as he directs us to play a different tune?

- Does he gesture to the cross while offering his other hand to lead us there?
- Look, as he uses one hand to gesture heavenward, calling for stronger voices and sounds of praise, while cupping his other hand around his ear to emphasize the point.
- Look again, as our actions bring a look of disappointment to the Savior's face.
- Do you realize *this* Director can continue to lead while his children sit on his lap, as he draws us to himself to confess our sins and receive his forgiveness?

And our Conductor's most important gesture of all? The opening of his arms wide in the surrender of love as his hands are nailed to a cross with Roman nails. With deep pain obvious on his face, he brought the first movement to a close a millennium ago, as with a loud voice he sang heavenward, "It is finished!" And then, in his Resurrection, he gestured us to walk forward into a new life in him!

> *Into your hand I commit my spirit;*
> *you have redeemed me, O LORD, faithful God.*
> *Psalm 31:5*

Prayer suggestion: Lord, you are my Song. I want to express my praise and thanks to you in new ways day by day. Let me see, really see, your face and recognize your direction as you lead and guide me. Amen.

Day 30

Concertmaster

Praise God as you read Colossians 3:1–4.

Concertmaster: The first violin in an orchestra

What an honor to be the concertmaster! First-chair violin in the orchestra; second in command, as it were, only to the conductor. Violinists in almost every orchestra set as their goal the honor of being chosen first violin.

But what about the violin player in the chair next to the concertmaster? Yes, the one playing second fiddle? Does she gladly accept that position, or will bitterness and jealousy grow within her?

How do you respond when asked by God to play second fiddle? You won't get the acclaim, the fame, or the attention the concertmaster receives. But without you, God's orchestra wouldn't sound the same. His people need your gifts! Your presence is vitally important, whether you are the concertmaster or in the back row of the violin section. When you set your thoughts on serving God in the best ways you know how in whatever seat he's assigned to you, your heart won't have space to harbor jealousy or nurse bitterness.

Consider these individuals chosen by God to play second fiddle in his kingdom's work:

- Aaron and Hur, who played second fiddle to Moses (Exodus 17:8–16)
- Naomi, second fiddle to Ruth (Ruth 1)
- Nathan, second fiddle to David (2 Samuel 12:1–23)
- Baruch, second fiddle to Jeremiah (Jeremiah 36:32)
- Barnabas, second fiddle to the apostles (Acts 4:36)
- Silas, second fiddle to Paul (Acts 16–17)
- Timothy, second fiddle to Paul (1 Timothy 4:11–16; 2 Timothy 1:1–7)

Set your minds on things that are above.
Colossians 3:2

Prayer suggestion: Pray for the second fiddle players you know who humbly serve the Lord with joy.

Day 31

Ensemble

Praise God as you read Luke 2:8–14.

Ensemble: The performance of either all instruments of an orchestra or voices in a chorus

Nothing stirred for most of the night. One man yawned and soon, as though that yawn was contagious, two others found themselves doing the same. They spent one evening after another, each one just like the last and like the one before that . . . until something turned their world upside down!

Like a thief in the night—unexpected and unannounced—God peeled back the very fabric of the universe. An angel appeared in the night sky—an angel reflecting the glory of the Godhead and bringing daylight where there once was darkness. One voice pierced the stillness:

Do not be afraid, for behold, I bring you good tidings of great joy which will be to all people. For there is born to you this day in the city of David a Savior, who is Christ the Lord. And this will be the sign to you: You will find a Babe wrapped in swaddling cloths, lying in a manger.

Luke 2:10–12 NKJV

The stunned shepherds stood (or knelt!) in awe when a great choir next appeared—an ensemble from heaven! As the heavens opened, the voices of myriad angels joined to glorify God. *Forte* was likely scrawled over the score. The angelic choir held nothing back:

> *Glory to God in the highest,*
> *And on earth peace,*
> *good will toward men!*
>
> Luke 2:14 NKJV

Take it in, my friends! Heaven's ensemble sent to earth! An angel choir larger than we can imagine praising God in unison—maybe in harmony—but in perfect praise, nevertheless.

Come together, people of God! Join the ensemble in a crescendo of praise to our Savior! Glory to God in the highest! Praise to the Lord of lords and King of kings—the world's Savior, born in Bethlehem and reborn in our hearts by the power of the Holy Spirit.

A Savior, who is Christ the Lord.
Luke 2:11

Prayer suggestion: Glory to you, O God; praise and adoration be yours! The ensemble of your people, gathered around your Word, lift our voices in a never-ending song of praise to you! Amen and amen!

Day 32

Finale

Praise God as you read 2 Timothy 4:7–8.

Finale: Movement or passage that concludes the musical composition

If Paul were a musician he might have described his finale this way:

I have played the entire piece, I have reached the final measure, I have stayed on key.

Instead, Paul used the image of an athlete, a runner, as he spoke of the finale written in large letters over his life:

I have fought the good fight, I have finished the race, I have kept the faith. Henceforth there is laid up for me the crown of righteousness which the Lord, the righteous judge, will award to me on that Day, and not only to me but also to all who have loved his appearing.
2 Timothy 4:7–8

I recently heard a pastor preach on this text, and he presented it in an entirely new insight. As Paul summarizes his faith walk in one sentence, he then points us forward to the gift of heaven and the victory crown of righteousness waiting for him. Did you notice Paul doesn't blindly hope for a crown of righteousness? Instead, he states that his crown *is* there. The Lord *will* award it to him. He has no doubt. Christ's death on the cross has brought forgiveness for all his sins and, by the grace of God, Paul has received the very righteousness of Jesus Christ himself.

But Paul doesn't stop there. He says the reward of heaven and a crown of righteousness await all who long for Christ's reappearing. The Lord *will* award them to us on that Day!

What a great *note* to end on. When we reach our finale, we can say, "I have played the entire piece, I have reached the final measure, and by the grace of Christ I have stayed on key! A crown of righteousness *does* await me in heaven!"

There is laid up for me the crown of righteousness, which the Lord, the righteous judge, will award to me on that Day, and not only to me but also to all who have loved his appearing.
2 Timothy 4:8

Prayer suggestion: Savior Jesus, our Song, we find such comfort in knowing you have saved us from an eternity without you and given us the crown of righteousness you won for us. It is ours, now, by grace through faith in you! I'll praise you forever! Amen!

Day 33

Encore

Praise God as you read Revelation 5:11–14.

Encore: A piece of music played at the end of a recital in response to the audience's enthusiastic reaction to a performance, shown by continuous applause

Day 1 in this book includes the following words concerning all who take part in these devotions:

Prayers arise before God's throne of grace, asking that the Holy Spirit work through his Word in this devotional to strengthen faith and create lives that sing praise—a crescendo of praise—to Jesus, our Song and Salvation.

I pray the praise you offer to our Savior has grown dramatically as he has continued to sing his song of salvation to you. Jesus, your Song, plays an eternal melody of grace daily within your life. May you offer your Savior encore after encore in praise of his amazing love—Father, Son, and Holy Spirit!

The LORD is my strength and song, and is become my salvation.
Psalm 118:14 KJV

Shout your praises to GOD, everybody!
Let loose and sing! Strike up the band!

Round up an orchestra to play for GOD,
Add on a hundred-voice choir.

Feature trumpets and big trombones,
Fill the air with praises to King GOD.

Let the sea and its fish give a round of applause,
With everything living on earth joining in.

Let ocean breakers call out, "Encore!"
And mountains harmonize the finale—
A tribute to GOD when he comes.
Psalm 98:4–9 THE MESSAGE

Bravo, GOD, Bravo!
Everyone join the great shout: Encore!
In awe before the beauty, in awe before the might.

Bring gifts and celebrate,
Bow before the beauty of GOD,
Then to your knees—everyone worship!
Psalm 96:7–9 THE MESSAGE

Prayer suggestion: Let the praise continue and never end—a crescendo of praise to Jesus, our Song—reverberating throughout our lives, throughout all creation! Bravo, God! We applaud your greatness! Encore! Encore! Amen and alleluia!

Days 34-35
Time for Reflection
Instruments of Praise

Which passages of praise in Scripture have had the greatest influence in your life as a music lover, musician, and/or a child of God? Read them again now. Then think about the truths that the Holy Spirit has impressed on your heart as you consider Jesus as your Song. Also pray, asking how you might share the joy of the Lord with someone.

The LORD is my strength and song, and is become my salvation.

Psalm 118:14 KJV

Praise the LORD!

Praise God in his sanctuary;
  praise him in his mighty heavens!
Praise him for his mighty deeds;
  praise him according to his excellent greatness!

Praise him with trumpet sound;
  praise him with lute and harp!
Praise him with tambourine and dance;
  praise him with strings and pipe!
Praise him with sounding cymbals;
  praise him with loud clashing cymbals!
Let everything that has breath praise the LORD!

Praise the LORD!

Psalm 150